annabelle cooks healthy

annabelle white

PENGUIN BOOKS

For all cooks who try hard to improve the quality of their own life by 'living healthy' for both themselves and their families – this book is for you. You deserve a pat on the back . . . we are all the better for it!

annabelle cooks
healthy

contents

PENGUIN BOOKS
Published by the Penguin Group
Penguin Group (NZ), 67 Apollo Drive, Rosedale,
North Shore 0632, New Zealand (a division of
Pearson New Zealand Ltd)

Penguin Group (USA) Inc., 375 Hudson Street,
New York, New York 10014, USA

Penguin Group (Canada), 90 Eglinton Avenue
East, Suite 700, Toronto, Ontario, M4P 2Y3,
Canada (a division of Pearson Penguin Canada
Inc.)

Penguin Books Ltd, 80 Strand, London, WC2R
0RL, England

Penguin Ireland, 25 St Stephen's Green, Dublin
2, Ireland (a division of Penguin Books Ltd)

Penguin Group (Australia), 250 Camberwell
Road, Camberwell, Victoria 3124, Australia (a
division of Pearson Australia Group Pty Ltd)

Penguin Books India Pvt Ltd, 11, Community
Centre, Panchsheel Park, New Delhi – 110 017,
India

Penguin Books (South Africa) (Pty) Ltd, 24
Sturdee Avenue, Rosebank, Johannesburg 2196,
South Africa

Penguin Books Ltd, Registered Offices: 80
Strand, London, WC2R 0RL, England

First published by Penguin Group (NZ), 2004
This edition published by Penguin Group (NZ),
2008
1 3 5 7 9 10 8 6 4 2

Copyright © Annabelle White, 2008

The right of Annabelle White to be identified as
the author of this work in terms of section 96 of
the Copyright Act 1994 is hereby asserted.

Photography by Kieran Scott
Designed and Typeset by Pindar New Zealand
(Egan Reid)
Printed in China through Bookbuilders, Hong
Kong

ISBN 978 014 300882 8

A catalogue record for this book is available
from the National Library of New Zealand.

www.penguin.co.nz

Acknowledgements

A cookbook is always a team effort, so many thanks to my assistant
Nicola Hudson for getting really involved and enthusiastic about this
project. Thanks also to photographer Kieran Scott for being such a
professional delight to work with and for producing such delicious
compositions.

A very special thank you to Mary Egan and the teams at Penguin and
Egan Reid for their outstanding efforts. Thank you all.

introduction

Healthy cooking and healthier living . . . the very words conjure up historic images of stern nutritionists with log books pointing accusingly at the groaning scales; or kaftan-wearing hippies munching seeds, preparing brown rice casseroles and tofu burgers. Today this couldn't be further from reality – living a healthier life is what we all strive for and need to work into our daily regime. The good news is that we all feel so much better for the effort.

Rather than seeing 'healthier living' as a short-term measure to help us lose a few kilos, lower cholesterol levels, or to cleanse our liver after a period of misuse, we should see it as a long-term goal to bring more fruit, vegetables, seafood, whole grains and low-fat dairy products into our daily menu, as well as consider other 'lighter' cooking options.

The nutritional information in the media has been constant – we all know that grilled chicken is much better for us than deep-fried; steamed vegetables are far superior to fries; and sushi is better than potato crisps. What has evolved is that we now have choices: we can choose to go for healthy or for healthier variations on a theme. We can take our favourite dishes and 'lighten' them or select steamed or grilled options that truly celebrate lighter eating. In this cookbook we have taken some traditional favourites such as Mussel Chowder (page 42) and Glazed Lemon and Buttermilk Cake (page 34), and made them healthier with equally, if not superior, results than the original higher-fat option.

While this is not rocket science, an interesting development took place while preparing this book. In the process of developing all these delicious recipes – and in some cases new ingredients like smoked mussels and oysters, and lite crème fraîche – we started to really enjoy the new flavours, tastes and healthier options. My assistant, Nicola Hudson, and I started a walking regime, and opted to steam and grill our food as a matter of choice, and we have now become converts to this healthier lifestyle.

Rather than seeing it as a punishment for earlier excesses, we found the new regime had us hooked, and we have become a little fanatical in the process. We have both become a little obsessed with our favourite kitchen appliances. In my kitchen, using a juicer is my favourite daily ritual – and I also customise juices for visiting friends and family. A quick glance at their faces or general disposition and I know if they need a cleansing juice like carrot, spinach and ginger, or a more substantial, antioxidant-rich blueberry smoothie. Nicola's busy kitchen has a steamer going all day – she loves the resultant purity of flavour and the ease of use of this versatile piece of equipment.

I carry small cans of tuna in my handbag at all times when travelling, and if other snack options look high in fat, all I need is a bread roll and my can of tuna and I have a snack with great flavour and a superb source of protein. My fridge has pottles of mussels for making pasta, risotto, fritters or chowder – again excellent protein and a valuable source of zinc for normal growth and wound healing.

Enjoy these pages of recipes and food information. Get creative with your appliances and reap the benefits of healthier cooking – you will wonder why you didn't do it years ago!

Annabelle White
Auckland

start the day

beetroot, carrot and orange juice

Beetroot has a very high antioxidant content (beta-carotene and vitamin C) and helps fight off infection; it also contains vitamin B, folic acid, calcium, iron, manganese, magnesium, phosphorus and potassium.

1 beetroot (trim the roots, do not peel)
2 carrots (do not peel or slice)
1 orange, cut in half

Place all the ingredients in a juicer in the order given and process.

Some people prefer to peel the orange before placing in the juicer – try it with the skin on, or if you like less peel or pith (which can be bitter), adjust accordingly.

apple, carrot and celery juice

The beta-carotene in carrots has beneficial effects on the respiratory and digestive systems, and for skin, and is vital for building strong teeth, hair and bones. It is also believed to lead to improved night vision and healthy eyes.

2 apples (do not peel or core)
2 carrots (do not peel or slice)
1 stalk celery

Place all the ingredients in a juicer and process.

apple, lime and kiwifruit juice

Limes and other citrus fruits are renowned for their high levels of the antioxidant vitamin C, which helps white blood cells fight infection, boosts immunity and maintains mental alertness and retentive memory.

Juicing an apple a day is good for your health. A London study found that eating at least five apples a week may improve lung function, thanks to the powerful antioxidant called quercetin that protects lungs from the effects of pollution and cigarette smoke.

2 apples (do not peel or core)
¼ fresh lime (skin on)
2 kiwifruit (skin on)

Place all the ingredients in a juicer and process.

green juice

A perfect drink to keep you fighting fit – the spinach gives a real boost of iron.

2–3 bulbs fennel, quartered
small bunch parsley
1 large handful spinach
1 large cucumber, cut into chunks

Place all the ingredients in a juicer, then pour into chilled glasses. Drink as soon as possible.

Eating 8 to 10 servings of fruits and vegetables a day can lower your risk of developing cancer. Research suggests that foods rich in vitamin A (such as carrots, red and yellow vegetables and green leafy vegetables) are especially protective for women, as this nutrient helps maintain the ovarian tissues that are most susceptible to cancer.

tips on juicing

Whenever you make a juice, try to drink it as soon as possible. The nutritional experts say the sooner you drink the juice, the better it is for your body.

You can add a generous slurp of plain unsweetened yoghurt to any of these juices to give them a smoother and creamier flavour, if desired. With the addition of yoghurt you are getting the bonus of calcium and protein in a low-fat option. You can also add low-fat milk for great taste and lower fat.

Try a variety of ingredients in a juicer. Remember – you don't have to peel and skin many fruits, so it's simple and easy. Don't forget to wash the fruit first.

When you first start juicing, try apple as a base – it gives a sweetness and a light body to any juice.

Rinse out your juicer attachments after use. I don't place the equipment in the dishwasher – a quick rinse out and get ready for more juicing!

left: beetroot, carrot and orange juice
back right: apple, lime and kiwifruit juice
front: apple, carrot and celery juice

spirulina smoothie

1 cup low-fat milk
1 banana, chopped
½ cup fruit yoghurt
⅓ cup pineapple juice
1 tbsp spirulina powder

Place the first 3 ingredients in a blender and blend well. Add the final 2 ingredients and process until smooth.

Spirulina powder is always best added as the last ingredient to a smoothie.

fruit salad smoothie

1 cup fruit juice
1 banana, chopped
1 orange, peeled and separated into
   segments
½ cup low-fat milk
3–4 tbsp fruit yoghurt

Place the first 3 ingredients in a blender and blend well. Add the remaining ingredients and process until smooth.

Smoothies are a fun, healthy way to approach breakfast for people on the move who want great flavour plus health benefits. Experiment with different flavours of yoghurt, milk and fruit.

pawpaw smoothie

¼ pawpaw, seeded and diced
1 cup low-fat milk
3 tbsp plain unsweetened yoghurt
2 fresh apricots or 4 apricot halves
   (canned)

Place all the ingredients in a blender and process until smooth.

Pawpaw is excellent for the digestive system.

blueberry banana smoothie

2 cups low-fat milk
½ banana, chopped
½ cup frozen blueberries
125 g fruit yoghurt

Place the first 2 ingredients in a blender and blend well. Add the berries and yoghurt and process until smooth.

Frozen berries make the smoothie much thicker.

breakfast smoothie

½ cup bran cereal
1 cup low-fat milk
½ banana, chopped
125 g yoghurt

First process the cereal with a little of the milk to blend well. Add remaining ingredients and process until smooth.

Remember, if you are using a low-fat milk product for children, add a scoop of ice cream to give them the fat they need for growing bodies. You can also add a tablespoon of wheatgerm, if desired.

Smoothies are a great way to make a substantial drink in seconds. Take your favourite fruit, place it in a blender, add a generous slurp of yoghurt and top with low-fat milk, and you have a complete meal in a glass. Smoothies contain fibre, vitamins, protein, calcium; they taste good and are easy to digest. From breakfast on-the-go to an afternoon snack, smoothies are only limited by your imagination.

front: blueberry banana smoothie
right: fruit salad smoothie

buttermilk waffles

When it comes to breakfast, believe what your mother always said – having a substantial breakfast is important to your health and well-being. Studies have shown that people who eat breakfast live longer. They also have more energy by mid-morning, particularly if protein is included. A serving of fruit provides the first of your fruit and vegetable requirements for the day. Think 'healthy and easy' and you will enhance your whole day.

buttermilk waffles

Make this mixture ahead of time and then just preheat a waffle maker – your family will love the results. Top with natural yoghurt and diced fresh fruit.

Cultured buttermilk is low-fat – only 0.8% – and provides protein and calcium for growing bodies. The advantage of buttermilk is that the natural lactic acid in the buttermilk reacts with the rising agent and makes these waffles super-moist and very appealing.

MAKES 10 WAFFLES
2 large eggs
1 cup cultured buttermilk
¾ cup low-fat milk
100 ml oil
2 cups self-raising flour
1½ tsp cinnamon
¼ cup sugar

Mix the first 4 ingredients together in you're a blender or food processor, then add flour, cinnamon and sugar.

Blend well, cover and let mixture stand (if possible) for 30 minutes before using.

Place ¼ cup of the mixture at a time in the heated waffle maker.

Serve with yoghurt and diced fresh fruit. Pawpaw, kiwifruit and banana are all superb with the creamy yoghurt and the chewy, buttery texture of the waffles.

savoury waffles

Simply remove the sugar and cinnamon from the previous basic recipe and add ½ onion, finely chopped; 3 tbsp chopped parsley; and ½ cup grated lite cheese. Cook as per instructions and top with slow-roasted tomatoes, a spoonful of cottage cheese with chives and garlic, and a spoonful of tuna in spring water (drained). Season with salt and pepper.

slow-roasted tomatoes

By using your non-stick frypan on a low heat and covering it with the lid, you can achieve great slow-roasted tomatoes. Spray the pan with olive oil spray and place the tomatoes, cut in half (cut-side down), in the pan and cook slowly until soft and golden in colour. Turn over and sprinkle with sea salt and herbs and cook until they reach the desired degree of softness. Long slow cooking is necessary. Do not worry too much about appearance – they will soften and lose shape – but the flavour is just superb, and with the combined benefits of a little olive oil and the non-stick frypan you are getting maximum flavour, minimal fat and all that goodness.

bircher muesli and fresh fruit

With a juicer sitting on your bench, you can also use it for recipes as well as for straight juicing. Here we juiced some fresh apples and poured the juice straight onto the rolled oats – now that has to be good for you!

SERVES 4
2 cups rolled oats
1½ cups fresh apple juice
2 apples, skin left on and grated
1½ cups plain unsweetened yoghurt
1 tbsp honey or maple syrup
2 tbsp toasted chopped almonds
½ cup blueberries (fresh or frozen)

Place the rolled oats and the apple juice in a bowl, cover and leave overnight in the fridge. Next morning, add the grated apple, yoghurt, honey or maple syrup, and mix well. Spoon into bowls and top with nuts and blueberries.

Organic unsweetened yoghurt is deliciously creamy and flavoursome, as well as providing a good source of calcium and vitamins. Yoghurt contains 'friendly' bacteria that, according to a growing amount of evidence, may stimulate the cells that fight bacteria and increase the gamma-interferon, an antiviral agent. Medical research found that people who ate yoghurt had 25% fewer colds than those who didn't!

creamy old-fashioned porridge

If the thought of getting up in the morning to make your beloved family a bowl of porridge each is just too hard, then consider placing these simple ingredients in you're a slow cooker the night before and you will be delighted to wake up to the aroma of cinnamon wafting through the house. After breakfast, simply soak the container while you are at work and that night remake another pot for the next morning.

SERVES 2–3
1 cup rolled oats
2 cups low-fat milk
1 cup water
½ tsp cinnamon
1 tsp salt

Mix all the ingredients in the bowl of the slow cooker and cook on low for 3–4 hours.

It's smart to leave the cooker on a timer to turn on at the appropriate time during the night.

You can add dried fruit like raisins or Craisins (dried sweetened cranberries) to the mix if desired.

Porridge cooked in this way needs almost no brown sugar on top. A little dash of apple syrup or a very small amount of liquid honey is a real treat.

bircher muesli and fresh fruit

easy scrambled eggs

Making scrambled eggs is so simple and healthy with a non-stick frypan as you need very little butter.

The culinary experts say strain the eggs before you cook them – this results in a creamy and tender texture.

SERVES 3–4
8 large eggs
2 tbsp low-fat milk
2 tbsp chopped parsley
salt and freshly ground black pepper
1 tbsp butter

In a medium bowl, whisk the eggs to combine. Add the milk, parsley, salt and pepper, and stir to combine. In the non-stick frypan, melt the butter gently, then add the egg mixture using a heat-resistant spoon, stirring constantly until the eggs begin to set. Stir for 3 more minutes, or until the eggs are very creamy. Serve immediately.

We served these on wholegrain toast, topped with red salmon.

A frypan can do the usual pan-frying, shallow-frying and sautéing, but it can also do some surprising things like baking a cake, or roasting a chicken or leg of lamb. Cooking times may take a little longer than in a conventional oven, but this is a great option for the bach, in the caravan, or if you live in a small unit – or if you simply don't want to heat up the oven.

easy scrambled eggs

spanish eggs for a crowd

This is a perfect start to the day for friends and family. Encourage one helper to 'get busy' with the juicer, and another to heat rolls or make toast, while you focus on this fabulous egg dish. The topping of tuna gives it a more brunch-like feel and the addition of protein without the fat makes good sense.

SERVES 4–6
5 tbsp oil
½ onion, chopped
9 large eggs, at room temperature
3 tbsp lite crème fraîche
salt and freshly ground black pepper
3 tbsp parsley, chopped
100 g spinach, washed and sliced
100 g mushrooms, sliced
2 × 210 g cans tuna in spring water, drained
½ red capsicum, thinly sliced

Heat the oil in a non-stick frypan over a moderate heat; add the onion and cook until translucent. In a bowl, mix eggs and crème fraîche together with salt and pepper, parsley and spinach. When the onions are cooked, add the mushrooms. When the mushrooms are softened, add the egg mixture to the pan. Place the lid on and cook until the mixture has just set. Remove lid, sprinkle the tuna and capsicums over the top, and place the lid back on the frypan to heat through. To serve, season again with salt and pepper if desired.

You can also add diced smoked chicken with the capsicums.

spanish eggs for a crowd

warm fruit salad

Don't think a wok is just for a quick stir-fry or curry; you can use it at breakfast for this great warm fruit salad to serve with Buttermilk Waffles (see page 15) or to top Creamy Old-fashioned Porridge (see page 16).

SERVES 3–4

800 g canned lite fruit (peaches, apricots or pears, or a mix), plus fruit syrup
2 tsp cornflour
2 tbsp cold water
½ cup fruit juice
1 cup frozen berries

Heat the wok. Strain the fruit syrup from the can of fruit into the wok and bring to the boil. Blend the cornflour and water together and stir into the fruit syrup; cook until thickened.

Add canned fruit and cook for 5 minutes. Add some of the fruit juice at this time if the mixture needs it. Add remaining fruit juice and frozen berries, heat through and you are ready to serve.

If you want more potassium – add a sliced banana just prior to serving.

Use a juicer to give you fresh apple or orange juice or a combination of both.

Serve with fruit yoghurts.

potatoes with lite sour cream and sweet chilli sauce

These grilled potatoes are great any time of the day but are particularly delicious at breakfast with eggs. You can use lite sour cream or unsweetened yoghurt as the base for the chilli sauce. This sauce is equally delicious served with grilled seafood and chicken. Even mussels cooked on the grill sparkle with this healthy sauce.

SERVES 6

1 kg potatoes, peeled
1 tbsp olive oil
mixed herb seasoning (optional)
2 tsp sea salt
freshly ground black pepper

SAUCE:

⅓ cup sweet Thai chilli sauce
⅔ cup lite sour cream or plain unsweetened yoghurt
2 tbsp finely chopped fresh coriander

Preheat a countertop grill for 3–5 minutes on medium setting. Cut potatoes in half lengthways and place in a bowl. Toss with oil, mixed herb seasoning, and salt and pepper. Cook potatoes on the grill for approximately 10 minutes or until tender.

To make the sauce, combine all the ingredients in a small bowl. Place bowl on a platter with hot potato wedges to one side.

A countertop grill is ideal for this recipe. If you like a rasher of bacon as well, you can simply cook it on the sloping grill plate; the fat drains away and the non-stick grill plates are easy to clean.

Eat eggs for your health. Eggs, along with colourful fruits and leafy green vegetables, contain large amounts of lutein, which helps fight macular degeneration and cataracts.

moving on
to brunch

the simplest kedgeree ever

the simplest kedgeree ever

Kedgeree has become very fashionable as a breakfast option in fancy B&B establishments worldwide. When you tire of eggs and pancakes, consider kedgeree. And of course, it makes a great Sunday lunch option or, after a busy day, a perfect Sunday supper with a green salad. It is both light and satisfying.

SERVES 2
1 cup long grain rice
2 eggs
1 tbsp olive oil
1 small onion, finely chopped
2 tsp curry paste
210 g can red salmon (do not drain)
85 g can smoked mussels, drained
2 small tomatoes, diced
3 tbsp chopped parsley
salt and freshly ground black pepper
juice of 1 lemon

Cook the rice as per your usual method. Hard-boil the egg. Let cool, then quarter.

In a non-stick frypan, heat the oil gently, add the onions and cook over a moderate heat. Stir in curry paste and, when aromatic, add the cooked rice, salmon plus the liquid from the can, smoked mussels, tomatoes and parsley and season with salt and pepper. Top with eggs.

Drizzle with a little lemon juice prior to serving.

salmon cakes

Another super-simple recipe that combines leftover mashed potatoes and a can of red salmon to make a filling and great-tasting savoury cake. By using a countertop grill, you can prepare these family favourites in a healthy way. Serve with a Tomato Salsa (page 36) or the Sweet Chilli Sauce on page 22.

SERVES 4
210 g can salmon, drained and flaked
2 cups mashed potato (not too wet)
2 spring onions, finely chopped
2 tbsp finely chopped parsley
1 large egg, lightly beaten
salt and freshly ground black pepper
½ cup breadcrumbs for coating
olive oil

In a large bowl combine the salmon, potato, spring onions, parsley, egg and salt and pepper.

Divide into 8 equal portions and form into balls, then flatten. Roll in breadcrumbs. Place patties on a plate covered with plastic wrap and refrigerate for 1–2 hours.

Preheat your grill on a medium setting for 3–5 minutes. Spray grill with olive oil spray. Cook 4 patties at a time for 5–7 minutes, or until crispy and golden and hot in the centre. Use a heatproof spatula to remove the patties. Halfway through cooking you may want to respray the grill plates to prevent patties from sticking.

Serve with scrambled eggs for breakfast or with a salad for brunch.

Wild Canadian red salmon contains those valuable and essential omega-3 fatty acids that keep our cardiovascular system healthy. Wild salmon has less risk of possible contamination from dyes, antibiotics and growth hormones.

basic pizza dough

Once you have tried this recipe you will be hooked. It is so simple and delicious.

MAKES 2 LARGE PIZZA BASES
1 tsp active dry yeast
⅔ cup warm water
2 cups plain flour
1 tsp salt
1 tsp oregano
1 tsp crushed garlic
olive oil

Place the yeast in measured warm water, stirring until the yeast dissolves. Leave for 5 minutes. In a large bowl, place flour, salt, oregano and garlic, then add dissolved yeast. Mix until combined thoroughly. Form dough into a large ball and place in a bowl that has been lightly oiled. Turn the dough to the top so the oiled side is exposed. Cover and place in a warm, draught-free area for 2 hours or until doubled in size. This mix can be left overnight.

After this resting period, push dough down and knead gently on a lightly floured surface. Divide the dough in half, then stretch and roll out each half to about 20 cm in circumference. You do not want the pizza to be too thin. Place dough on pizza trays (sprayed with olive oil) or straight onto an oven tray (sprayed with olive oil).

smoked mussel mini pizzas

SERVES 4
1 basic pizza dough
4 tbsp tomato relish
85 g can smoked mussels, drained
1 red capsicum, deseeded and thinly sliced
1 yellow capsicum, deseeded and thinly sliced
2 spring onions, finely chopped
2 cups grated tasty cheese
2 cups salad greens
freshly grated Parmesan to serve

Preheat oven to 180°C. Divide the pizza dough into 4 portions and form into 4 pizza bases. Place bases on a greased baking tray. Spread 1 tbsp of relish on each pizza. Divide the mussels between the 4 pizzas, then top with capsicum slices, spring onions and grated cheese. Bake for 15 minutes.

To serve, place pizza on a plate and top with salad greens and Parmesan.

smoked mussel mini pizzas

bitter limeade

With your blender you can make a superb, refreshing citrus drink that is the perfect companion to the mini pizzas.

SERVES 4
5 juicy limes, each cut into 8 pieces
1 cup sugar
1 cup water

Put the limes, including peel, in a blender with the sugar and water. Pulse 3 or 4 times until all the lime is chopped. Don't overdo it or the drink will be too bitter.

Sieve the mixture over a bowl, squeezing the chopped limes to get as much juice out as possible. Top with water and ice.

Don't throw away the peel of lemon, limes, oranges and grapefruit. A recent University of Arizona study concluded that eating citrus peel is good for your health and can reduce the risk of skin cancer by as much as 30%.

something
wonderful
with coffee

best fruit muffins

Keep a container of cultured buttermilk in your fridge at all times – it will last for ages, unopened, and can instantly transform your baking.

MAKES 16–18 LARGE OR 40 MINI
4 cups self-raising flour
¾ cup sugar
2 tsp cinnamon
1 tsp lemon zest
1½ cups cultured buttermilk
4 large eggs, lightly beaten
75 ml vegetable oil
2 cups diced fresh or frozen fruit (or
  you can use fresh or frozen berries)
mixture of cinnamon and sugar for
  dusting

Preheat oven to 180°C. Place the first 3 ingredients in a large bowl. Add the next 4 ingredients, then the fruit and mix very gently (do not over-mix). Place mixture in greased muffin pans and top with a light dusting of cinnamon and sugar. Fan bake for approximately 20 minutes for large muffins and 15 minutes for mini muffins, or until a skewer inserted comes out clean.

We made fresh apple muffins and drizzled the fruit with a little apple syrup to intensify the apple experience.

We have made these muffins successfully using as little as 25 ml of vegetable oil, but the best results came with using a little more.

Using cultured buttermilk in your baking is a culinary bonus. The lactic acid in the buttermilk reacts with the raising agent – such as baking powder or self-raising flour – and creates an extra-moist, soft result in scones, muffins, cakes or pancakes.

best fruit muffins

muesli slice

muesli slice

If you are craving a little something crunchy and sweet – why not opt for this healthy slice?

MAKES 32 PIECES
2 tbsp sesame seeds
1 tbsp sunflower seeds
¾ cup flour
¼ tsp baking powder
1½ cups rolled oats
¼ cup caster sugar
½ cup chopped dried apricots
½ cup sultanas
zest of 1 orange
150 g butter
2 tbsp honey

Preheat oven to 180°C. Line a lamington tin (27 cm × 17.5 cm) with baking paper, allowing the paper to hang over the sides. Heat a non-stick frypan to medium high. Cook sesame seeds and sunflower seeds, tossing occasionally, for 2 minutes or until lightly toasted. Cool.

Sift the flour and baking powder into a bowl and add the cooled sesame and sunflower seeds, oats, sugar, apricots, sultanas and orange zest.

Heat butter and honey in a saucepan on a medium heat and stir constantly until melted and well combined. Cool slightly, then pour over the flour mixture and mix until well combined. Spoon mixture into prepared tin, pressing down evenly using the back of a spoon. Bake for 20 minutes or until cooked through and golden brown. Remove and cool completely in tin. Slice to serve.

the best light gingerbread

With the help of cultured buttermilk you can transform this family favourite into something stellar! Try it warm from the oven with a cup of coffee, or serve warm with slow cooker fruit (see page 92) and lite crème fraîche mixed with a little chopped crystallized ginger.

SERVES 4–6
100 g butter
1 cup sugar
2 tbsp golden syrup
½ tsp salt
1 tsp cinnamon
½ tsp ground cloves
1 tsp ground ginger
1 large egg
2 cups flour
1 tsp baking soda
1 cup cultured buttermilk
1 tbsp grated lemon zest

Preheat the oven to 180°C. Line a loaf tin with baking paper.

Cream the butter, sugar and golden syrup. Add the salt, cinnamon, cloves and ginger and stir well. Beat in the egg. Sift the flour and baking soda together and add, alternately with the buttermilk, to the butter and sugar mixture, beginning and ending with the dry ingredients. Add lemon zest. Bake for 50–65 minutes depending on the depth of your loaf pan or until a skewer inserted comes out clean. Leave in pan for 5 minutes before removing.

glazed lemon and buttermilk cake

For many years I have been receiving mail from readers who simply love the Sour Cream Lemon Cake in my book, *Best Recipes*. This is a lighter variation on the same theme – you will be delighted with the refreshing lemon tang. This cake freezes well.

SERVES 6–8
150 g butter, softened
1 cup sugar
3 eggs
2 cups self-raising flour
pinch of salt
¾ cup cultured buttermilk
1 tbsp lemon zest
1 tbsp lemon juice

GLAZE:
juice of 1 lemon
1 tbsp lemon zest
¼ cup sugar

Preheat oven to 160°C. Butter a 20–cm baking tin.

Cream the butter and sugar. Beat in eggs one at a time. Fold in sifted flour and salt alternately with the buttermilk, lemon zest and juice, and combine gently. Pour mixture into baking tin and bake for 60 minutes or until a skewer inserted comes out clean. While cake is hot pour over the glaze.

To make the glaze, combine all the ingredients.

midday meals should be this good

corn fritters with tomato salsa

Corn fritters are a great solution for a weekend lunch or Sunday supper. Always popular with the whole family, try them with lightly cooked fresh corn when in season for great taste and texture.

SERVES 3–4

1 cup flour
1 tsp baking powder
½ cup soda water
2 eggs, lightly beaten
½ tsp salt
2 spring onions, finely chopped
3 tbsp finely chopped parsley
410 g can whole kernel corn, drained
**1 tsp fresh chilli (optional), deseeded
    and finely chopped**
light olive oil

Place the flour, baking powder, soda water, eggs and salt together in a bowl and mix well. Add the spring onions, parsley and corn, and chilli if using, and blend well. Heat oil in a non-stick frypan on a medium heat. Place spoonfuls of the mixture in the oil. Turn the fritters when golden (turn only once). Place fritters on kitchen paper towels to absorb any oil before serving.

tomato salsa

Instead of accompanying fritters with rich, creamy sauces, substitute fresh salsa such as this versatile tomato salsa. Not only is it better for you and will help you get your required servings of fruit and vegetables each day, but it also tastes amazing. You will shun cream sauces forever after sampling this one!

½ red onion, finely chopped
3 tomatoes, chopped
1 tsp fresh lime juice
½ cup chopped telegraph cucumber
1 tbsp chopped parsley
1 tbsp chopped mint
1 tbsp chopped coriander
1 tsp sweet Thai chilli sauce
salt and freshly ground black pepper
splash of avocado oil

Combine all the ingredients and serve with fritters.

corn fritters with tomato salsa

cook's tip

To peel tomatoes, make a cross in the base
of the tomato with a serrated knife. Place
in a bowl and pour over boiling water. Let
tomatoes sit in the water for 30 seconds.
The skin should now simply slip off.

peanut chicken soba salad

peanut chicken soba salad

The perfect lunch suggestion. Don't let the number of ingredients put you off – it's well worth the effort.

SERVES 4–6

1 tbsp rice vinegar
2 tbsp peanut oil
2 tsp low-sodium soy sauce
1 tsp honey
1 tsp chilli garlic sauce
pinch of salt
2 boneless chicken breasts, cooked
  and shredded
2 cups cooked soba noodles
1 cup grated carrot
½ cup sliced spring onions
¼ cup sliced red onion
¼ cup chopped fresh basil
2 tbsp chopped cashews
¼ cup thinly sliced red capsicums
¼ cup thinly sliced telegraph cucumber
2 tbsp peanuts
2–3 tbsp chopped coriander
lime wedges (optional)

Combine the first 6 ingredients with a whisk. Pour over chicken and let stand for 5 minutes. Add soba noodles and the next 7 ingredients to the chicken mixture and toss well. Sprinkle with peanuts and chopped coriander. Garnish with lime wedges.

You can either steam this chicken in a steamer or cook the chicken in a non-stick frypan in 2 cups of water (add a few peppercorns and a bay leaf). Bring the chicken and water to the boil, cover, then turn down the heat and let stand for 15 minutes or until chicken is cooked.

gazpacho with a twist

Gazpacho is a traditional Spanish soup crammed full of tomatoes, capsicum and cucumber – a delight for healthy eaters. Great flavours and a refreshingly cool starter that celebrates the summer garden – try it!

SERVES 2–4

6 ripe tomatoes, peeled
½ red onion, chopped
3 garlic cloves
½ cup water
½ cup chopped green capsicum
1 small cucumber, peeled and chopped
½ cup watercress (optional)
2 cups cultured buttermilk
salt and freshly ground black pepper
pinch of sugar (optional)
fresh chopped basil
1 tbsp chopped chives

Cook the tomatoes, red onion and garlic in water for 15 minutes. Remove from the heat and add the capsicum, cucumber and watercress. Put mixture through a food processor or blender (strain for finer texture). Add the buttermilk and season with salt and pepper to taste. (Add a pinch of sugar, if desired.) Serve in a bowl with a few ice cubes and garnished with basil and chives.

You could use a wok to cook the tomatoes, onions and garlic.

The cultured buttermilk gives this soup a refreshing, more luxurious edge to it – but it's all low-fat!

steamed dory fillets with fresh corn and green bean salad

All you have to do with the steamer is to fill it with water as per the instructions and switch it on – and you are ready to go. At our test kitchen we started steaming months ago and the steamer has not left the bench!

SERVES 4

2 ears fresh corn
12 gourmet baby potatoes
200 g fresh green beans
salt and freshly ground black pepper
450 g packet dory fillets (defrosted in
**   fridge, covered in paper towels)**
select a dressing from page 50 or
**   page 87 to drizzle over fish**
1 lime, to serve

Prepare your food steamer.

Remove the husks from the corn. Wash the potatoes (do not peel) and slice in half length-ways. Top and tail whole green beans. Season fish with salt and pepper.

Place the corn in the bottom tray of the steamer, cover with the lid and turn on for 30 minutes.

When finished remove the corn and leave to cool. Place potatoes in steamer in lower level, cover with lid and cook for 10 minutes. Then place beans in together with potatoes and cook for another 5 minutes. Place another steaming tray on top and lay fish on this. Cover and steam for 12 minutes.

Place the corn cob upright in a bowl and carefully shuck using a sharp knife. Reserve.

On warmed plates layer the potato slices, then green beans and corn. Top with fish, and drizzle with dressing. Serve with a slice of lime.

To defrost the frozen fish, simply pull the packet out of the freezer and leave to thaw in the bag in the fridge.

oriental fish fillets

With fish fillets and a countertop grill you can achieve great simple flavours in minutes with minimal effort.

SERVES 4

4 hoki fillets
2 tbsp honey
1 orange, juice and zest
3 cm piece fresh ginger, grated
olive oil

Place fish fillets on a plate. In a small jug combine honey, orange juice and zest, and grated ginger. Pour mixture over the fish and leave on a cool bench for 10 minutes or in the fridge for 20 minutes. Preheat the grill for 3–5 minutes on a medium setting and spray with olive oil. Cook the fish fillets for 5–6 minutes on the grill or until flaky.

Always remember to cook your fish medium rare as it will continue to 'cook' after it has been removed from the heat.

Serve this fish with Chilli Stir-fried Bok Choy (see page 76).

steamed dory fillets with fresh corn and green bean salad

mussel fritters

We couldn't stop eating these mussel fritters when we tested them. The slight vinegar/brine flavour from the mussels completely enhanced the fritter experience. Beware, these are highly addictive!

MAKES ABOUT 12 FRITTERS

2 × 375 g pottles garlic marinated mussels, drained and roughly chopped
1 cup flour
1 tsp baking powder
½ tsp salt
freshly ground black pepper
3 eggs
½ cup low-fat milk
2 spring onions, finely chopped
¼ cup chopped parsley
light olive oil

Place all the ingredients except oil in a bowl in the order given and mix gently, but well.

Pour light olive oil in a non-stick frypan and cook the fritters on a medium-hot heat. The fritters should be crisp and golden on one side before turning over and cooking the other side.

Serve with avocado salsa – follow the recipe for Tomato Salsa on page 36, replacing the tomato with finely diced avocado.

Seafoods, especially shellfish, are not often recommended as sources of iron but may in fact be equal to or have more iron than red meat. In addition, much of the iron in seafood is present in the organic form most easily absorbed by the body. Mussels and oysters are particularly rich in iron.

mussel chowder

This is a mouth-watering suggestion for lunch. Full of goodness and easy to eat, Mussel Chowder can be made in a wok or stockpot. It looks creamy but it's made with low-fat milk, so you can enjoy a big bowl without feeling any guilt.

SERVES 4–6

2 × 375 g pottles mussels
15 g butter
2 rashers low-fat bacon
1 red capsicum, finely chopped
1 small red onion, finely chopped
2 tbsp flour
1½ cups low-fat milk
1 cup fish stock
2 small potatoes, finely chopped
2 spring onions, finely chopped
1 cup whole kernel corn
4 tbsp finely chopped parsley

Drain the pottles of mussels, then roughly chop. Heat butter in the wok or large stockpot. Add bacon, capsicum and onion and cook on a medium heat for 5 minutes.

Add flour and cook for 1–2 minutes. Remove from the heat and gradually stir in milk and fish stock. Add potatoes and stir over a high heat until mixture boils and thickens.

Reduce heat, then add chopped mussels, spring onions, corn and parsley. Reheat mixture without boiling.

mussel fritters

greek salad with tuna

greek salad with tuna

When you order a tuna salad in the Mediterranean it often comes with sliced tomato, grated carrot and onion plus a bottle of olive oil and vinegar. This salad celebrates that delicious simplicity . . . enjoy!

SERVES 4–6

200 g feta, cubed
1 cup whole cherry tomatoes or 4–6 medium tomatoes, sliced
¾ cup pitted Kalamata olives
3 spring onions or ½ red onion, finely sliced
½ capsicum, deseeded and thinly sliced
shredded basil or oregano
1 gourmet lettuce
210 g can tuna in olive oil, drained

VINAIGRETTE:

1 tbsp lemon juice
4 tbsp olive oil
1 tsp wholeseed mustard
salt and freshly ground black pepper

Combine all salad ingredients gently in a bowl.

Combine vinaigrette ingredients together and mix well.

Pour vinaigrette over salad. Serve immediately with crusty bread.

tomato crème fraîche pasta sauce

Lite crème fraîche is a real bonus for the busy home cook. It has a wonderful nutty flavour but with less fat than regular crème fraîche. It still has all those beneficial crème fraîche qualities – you can acidulate with lemon juice or wine, and boil the sauce without fear of separation. Good news for busy cooks.

SERVES 4

250 g pasta shells or penne
olive oil
1 onion, chopped
2–3 cloves garlic, minced
3 rashers bacon, chopped
2–3 tbsp chopped fresh herbs (rosemary, fresh thyme, parsley)
250 g mushrooms, chopped
410 g can seasoned tomatoes (of your choice)
3 cups smoked diced chicken or diced ham
125 g lite crème fraîche
salt and freshly ground black pepper
grated Parmesan to serve
additional fresh herbs to serve

Cook pasta according to the directions on the packet. Drain and drizzle with oil to prevent the pasta from sticking. Scatter a few chopped herbs over the hot pasta.

In a non-stick frypan or wok, sauté the onion, garlic and bacon in a little olive oil until the onion is translucent. Add fresh herbs and mushrooms.

When the mushrooms are softened, add the tomatoes, diced chicken or ham and crème fraîche, and allow to heat through. Season with salt and pepper, then toss through the drained pasta. Serve with plenty of grated Parmesan and top with additional fresh herbs.

tuna, spinach and feta panini

To make this extra healthy, we did not spread the bread with butter, oil, spread or mayonnaise and it was still delicious – the spinach created moisture as it cooked and the feta melted into the tuna and provided a creamy base. A sandwich maker or grill does all the hard work for you. Avoid adding spreads as often it is only a matter of habit.

SERVES 2

½ cup washed and roughly chopped spinach

4 slices bread or 2 panini, sliced

½ cup drained tuna in spring water

½ cup crumbled feta

olive oil

Preheat your grill or sandwich maker.

Place the washed and dried spinach on 2 slices of bread, then the tuna and top with feta. Place another piece of bread on top and grill until golden brown. When you first use your grill, spray with olive oil and wipe with a paper towel. Use regularly and you won't need to add any more oil.

Remember: you are only limited by your imagination when it comes to panini. Why not try chargrilled peppers with mussels or shrimp; smoked chicken with rocket and Gruyère; tuna, olive, tomato and pesto. Even a simple ham and cheese sandwich turns out perfectly with the non-stick surface of a sandwich maker or grill. Always preheat the grill and these sandwiches will be ready in minutes.

tomato, mozzarella and pesto panini

A slightly richer version of a simple panini. Take away the oil and reduce the pesto if desired.

SERVES 1

2 slices thick bread

1 tbsp extra virgin olive oil

2 tbsp pesto

2 slices mozzarella

2 slices fresh tomato

small handful of mixed baby greens

Preheat the grill or sandwich maker. Brush 1 side of bread with olive oil. Lay the oiled slice down on a work surface and spread pesto on both slices.

Arrange the mozzarella, tomato and mixed greens on 1 bread slice. Top with the other bread slice and grill until golden and crunchy.

health tip

Steam your vegetables! A recent Spanish study found that fresh produce loses as much as 97% of its antioxidant properties when microwaved. The healthiest way to eat vegetables is steamed or raw.

tuna sandwich

tuna sandwich

Sometimes when you say the words 'tuna fish sandwich', people think of a soft white-bread sandwich with a hint of lettuce and the tuna dripping in mayonnaise. So we made an ultra-healthy tuna sandwich. If you wish, add a drizzle of olive oil dressing – it's up to you.

SERVES 4

4 large pieces of ciabatta or Turkish bread, cut in half horizontally
1–2 tbsp olive oil
2 tbsp lemon juice
185g can tuna in spring water, drained
1 garlic clove, cut in half
2 cups salad greens
2 tomatoes, sliced
salt and freshly ground black pepper
¼ red onion, sliced
½ carrot, grated
handful of sliced cheese

Place the bread on a board. Brush the bread with a light smear of olive oil. Squeeze the lemon juice over the tuna and place to one side. Take the garlic and smear all over the oil on the bread.

Assemble the sandwiches with salad greens, tomatoes, salt and pepper to taste, onion, tuna, carrot and cheese. Finish by placing the top on the sandwich.

Add sliced avocado, if desired. Hard-boiled eggs work equally well in this sandwich.

Tuna is a valuable source of omega-3 fatty acids which are beneficial to the heart and circulatory system. They lower blood cholesterol and blood pressure, and make the blood less sticky, thereby reducing the risk of heart disease and strokes. Some research suggests they can also help inflammatory conditions such as rheumatoid arthritis.

grilled fruit skewers with ginger syrup

This is a delicious option for a light fruit ending to a sandwich lunch. With a countertop grill you can easily prepare low-fat, warm fruit with a drizzle of ginger syrup. Serve with organic unsweetened yoghurt.

SERVES 4–6
GINGER SYRUP:
1 cup sugar
1 cup water
¼ cup peeled and thinly sliced fresh ginger

4 bananas, not overly ripe, unpeeled
4 peaches
1 small pineapple
1 pawpaw, ripe but not too soft

Combine the ginger syrup ingredients in a saucepan over a medium heat. Bring to the boil and simmer for 3 minutes. Remove from the heat, cool to room temperature, then strain. You can make this syrup in advance and refrigerate for up to 1 week.

Slice unpeeled bananas into 5-cm-long chunks and make a small slit in the peel. Quarter peaches, discarding the stone. Peel and core pineapple and cut into 5 cm chunks. Peel pawpaw, cut in half, discard seeds and cut flesh into 5 cm chunks.

Thread fruit onto 8 skewers or place chunks directly onto the hot grill. Brush lightly with ginger syrup. Grill until lightly browned, about 2 minutes each side. Brush again with ginger syrup and serve warm.

smoked oyster salad

All seafood provides high-quality protein and the essential amino acids, and is highly digestible.

Oysters have become famous as an extraordinarily concentrated source of zinc – an essential mineral in our diets. Other molluscs, such as mussels and crab, are also rich in zinc.

SERVES 2
3–4 cups salad greens
¼ cup thinly sliced red onion
½ cup sliced tomatoes
½ cup sliced cucumber
¼ cup toasted pine nuts
85 g smoked oysters, drained

Gently combine all the ingredients in a salad bowl and lightly drizzle with Fresh Herb Dressing (see below).

In this recipe we used smoked oysters but you can use any canned seafood. The salad is lightly dressed with my favourite herb dressing which I keep in my fridge and use every day to dress hot vegetables. Make the dressing in a blender or food processor.

fresh herb dressing

1 cup oil
⅓ cup white wine vinegar
squeeze of lemon juice
½ tsp salt
2 tsp honey or apple syrup
1–2 tsp freshly ground black pepper
2 tsp wholeseed mustard
3–4 garlic cloves, minced
1 tsp lemon zest
½ cup chopped parsley
½ cup chopped mint (or basil, oregano, thyme)

Place all the ingredients in the blender and process for a minute. Pour into a screw-top jar and refrigerate. The dressing is best made the day before it is to be used for the flavours to infuse.

Use this excellent dressing for different salads. It keeps for up to 10 days in a screw-top jar in the fridge. To revitalise the dressing, add fresh lemon juice.

smoked oyster salad

ratatouille, wok-style

This is one of my favourite summer dishes. Low in fat, simple to make and, when these vegetables are in season, so good for the budget. You can enjoy this ratatouille on toast for breakfast; served cold with salad and tuna; or hot over grilled chicken or fish. It can be a rustic sauce; a topping for pasta; part of an antipasto platter – and leftovers can be used in panini.

SERVES 4–6

1 tbsp oil

1 red onion, finely chopped

3 cloves garlic

fresh basil and thyme

500 g courgette, sliced

½ eggplant, cut into horizontal slices and then quartered

2 capsicums, deseeded and sliced

250 g mushrooms, sliced

3 large ripe tomatoes, roughly chopped

2 tsp balsamic vinegar

salt and freshly ground black pepper

Heat oil in your wok or frypan. Add the onion, garlic and a scattering of fresh herbs, then turn down the heat slightly so the onions cook very gently and become translucent and soft rather than coloured.

Add all the remaining vegetables and a little more of the fresh herbs. Cover and simmer gently until vegetables are tender (about 10–15 minutes). Do not rush this stew; the longer and more gentle the cooking, the sweeter the result.

Once the vegetables have cooked and are tender, add the balsamic vinegar and more fresh herbs. Season to taste with salt and pepper.

You may wish to add a pinch of sugar to this vegetable stew if the tomatoes are very acidic or not fully ripe.

Use a wok for rice dishes, stir-fries, curries, stews and deep-frying, and a food processor for quick slicing of vegetables.

crab cakes

SERVES 4
500 g crab meat, drained
4–5 slices white bread, grated
½ tbsp chopped parsley
½ tbsp chopped coriander
**¼ cup good quality commercial
    mayonnaise**
1 tbsp Dijon mustard
1 large egg
white pepper
1 cup very fine breadcrumbs
2 tbsp butter
1 lemon, cut into wedges

Place the crab meat, bread, parsley and coriander in a bowl. In another bowl, whisk together the mayonnaise, mustard and egg, seasoning with white pepper. Slowly pour the dressing into the crab meat mixture, using a fork to combine. Add just enough dressing to bind the mixture together.

Form the crab meat mixture into cakes using the palms of your hands and transfer to a plate. Cover with plastic wrap and place in the fridge for 1 hour.

Dip the crab cakes in breadcrumbs to coat. Heat butter in the a non-stick frypan over a medium heat and cook crab cakes until browned on one side. Turn only once, and cook until golden brown on the other side. Serve with wedges of lemon.

Try these delicious family favourites with a mixed green salad.

Panko (Japanese) breadcrumbs are delicious and worth searching out for this recipe.

health tip

Eat more fish! Recent research shows that omega-3 fatty acids may help regulate the mechanisms that allow bones to absorb calcium. Salmon, in particular, is an omega-3 rich food.

seafood risotto

seafood risotto

Full of seafood delights and so easy to prepare.

SERVES 4
1 tbsp olive oil
1 tsp salt
50 g butter
1 small onion, finely diced
340 g arborio rice
6 cups hot seafood stock
1 bunch asparagus spears, sliced
    on the diagonal
4 dory fillets, cut into slices
210 g can crab meat, drained
80 g can smoked mussels, drained
juice and zest of 1 lemon
salt and freshly ground black pepper
1 tbsp capers
fresh dill, chopped

Heat a non-stick frypan to a medium heat. Place the oil, salt and half the butter into the pan. Add onion and cook gently until onion is translucent. Add rice and stir for 2–3 minutes until rice is well coated. Add hot stock, a cup at a time, stirring constantly and making sure the stock is well absorbed before you add more. Continue adding stock for about 25 minutes. Add asparagus and sliced fish, and continue to add remaining stock for another 2 minutes or until the rice is al dente and creamy. Remove the saucepan from the heat, stir in remaining butter, crab meat, smoked mussels, lemon juice and zest. Season to taste with salt and pepper. Stir gently. Decorate with capers and chopped fresh dill to serve.

Most seafood is relatively low in total fat and high in polyunsaturated fatty acids. This gives it a clear health advantage. Most varieties of tin fish and all shellfish contain less than 5% fat in the raw muscle. The predominant polyunsaturated fatty acids in fish oils are the omega-3 variety, which are so beneficial for your health.

delicious vegetable pulp cake

You have several options with the remaining pulp from your juicer: you can add the pulp to a soup or stew, or make this super-easy cake that is cooked in the microwave. It takes minutes to make and cook, and for those who do not own a microwave then I have also included conventional cooking methods and times.

3 cups vegetable pulp
4 large eggs
1½ cups brown sugar
1 cup vegetable oil
2 tsp vanilla
2 cups flour
3 tsp cinnamon
3 tsp mixed spice
1½ tsp baking soda
¾ tsp salt

Place the first 5 ingredients in a large bowl and mix well. Sift in dry ingredients, and combine very gently. For the microwave, pour the mixture into a 20-cm plastic ring mould and cook on high for 18 minutes.

For a conventional oven, pour the mixture into a normal 20-cm tin and bake at 180°C for approximately 1 hour. Check after 50–55 minutes by inserting a skewer.

This cake can be served warm with spoonfuls of plain unsweetened yoghurt or lite crème fraîche.

banana vanilla pudding

Sometimes you just feel like a rich and creamy pudding after weeks of eating fresh fruit desserts – your grandmother's custard or milk pudding would be ideal. Here is a dessert that is low in fat and conjures up all those comforting memories!

SERVES 6
2 cups low-fat milk
3 large egg yolks
¼ cup sugar
¼ cup cornflour
pinch of salt
1 tsp vanilla essence
4 bananas, sliced thinly
crumbled biscuits or fresh berries to
   serve

In a wok bring 5–7 cm water to a simmer. In a large heatproof bowl, whisk together the first 5 ingredients. Place bowl in wok, to sit in simmering water. Cook, whisking until mixture thickens (allow about 6–9 minutes). Remove from heat and whisk in vanilla.

Place the sliced bananas in 6 ramekins and pour hot pudding over the sliced fruit. Smooth tops, submerging the bananas. Refrigerate for 1 hour, or ideally overnight, until set.

Garnish with crumbled biscuits, if desired, or fresh berries.

meringues

3 large egg whites (at room
   temperature)
180 g caster sugar
¼ tsp vanilla essence

Preheat the oven to 150°C. Line a baking tray with baking paper. Beat egg whites until stiff peaks form, then add sugar, a little at a time, while still beating. Beat in vanilla. Place spoonfuls of meringue onto a baking tray and bake for 45 minutes. Turn oven off, leaving the door ajar, and allow the meringues to cool completely in the oven. Store meringues in an airtight container lined with greaseproof paper.

Make meringues with leftover egg whites
and serve with plain unsweetened yoghurt
and fresh fruit instead of cream.

delicious vegetable pulp cake

steamed fruit pudding

Without a doubt this is the best fruit pudding I've ever made, and minus all the hassles of topping up water in a large pot on the stove. If you ever needed a reason to buy a slow cooker, this is it. It is unquestionably the best way to cook a fruit pudding. Simply cook for 7–9 hours on high and serve with lite crème fraîche or plain unsweetened yoghurt.

SERVES 12

500 g mixed fruit (I use sultanas, raisins and chopped apricots)
½ cup brown sugar
75 g butter
¼ cup freshly squeezed orange juice
2 tbsp brandy
1 tsp baking soda
2 eggs, lightly beaten
1 cup self-raising flour
1 tsp mixed spice

In a saucepan, combine mixed fruit, sugar, butter, orange juice and brandy. Heat until the butter is melted and the mixture begins to boil. Remove from the heat, allow to cool for 10–15 minutes, then add baking soda and allow to cool completely.

Grease and line the base of a 10-cup pudding bowl.

Add eggs to the cooled mixture and mix until well combined. Fold through flour and spice. Pour mixture into prepared bowl, cover with a double layer of foil and secure tightly with string. Cover with lid and place in a slow cooker with water coming halfway up the sides of the basin. Cover cooker and cook pudding on high for 7–9 hours.

If you want a delicious option, change the fruit mixture to include grated carrot and apple as well as dried fruit.

Serve with organic unsweetened fruit yoghurt for a rich creamy taste.

steamed fruit pudding

lemon mousse

This is a delicate, light mousse that everyone loves and it can easily be made in advance. Substitute the lemon for a lime when you can, and serve with a small wedge of the Glazed Lemon and Buttermilk Cake on page 34. To impress your friends with your next dessert, announce you have whipped up a 'trio of citrus'. Serve each guest a white plate with the mousse in a small bowl, a thin wedge of the lemon and buttermilk cake and a tiny dish of organic unsweetened yoghurt with a swirl of lemon curd. A small glass of chilled lemon liqueur (limoncello) will send them into convulsions of delight.

SERVES 4–6

4 eggs

1 tbsp unflavoured gelatin

¼ cup cold water

2 cups cultured buttermilk

¼ cup sugar

½ cup lemon juice

2 tbsp lemon zest

Separate the eggs while they are cold. Soften the gelatin for about 5 minutes in the cold water. In a saucepan over low heat, combine the egg yolks, buttermilk and sugar. Cook, stirring frequently, until thick and mixture coats the back of a spoon. Remove from the heat and add the gelatin, lemon juice and zest. Place the mixture in the fridge to cool – it will begin to congeal. When cool, beat the egg whites until stiff and fold into the mixture. Spoon mousse into ramekin dishes and refrigerate until ready to serve.

Cultured buttermilk is a product more similar to yoghurt than milk. It has a sour taste and a lumpy texture and is specially prepared using all natural ingredients. A culture is added to fresh low-fat milk, creating a distinctive flavour. It contains no artificial additives and no preservatives.

cook's tip

Before folding in the beaten egg whites, first stir 1 large spoonful of egg white into the mixture to lighten it, then fold in the balance. For an extra light mousse, you can use up to twice as many egg whites. Do not double the recipe. This mousse also freezes well.

pre-dinner —
why not serve
a healthy
antipasto
platter?

antipasto

Invest in a white platter and serve clusters of nibbles around the plate. A small pile of cherry tomatoes, a pile of mussels, salmon and crème fraîche dip, yoghurt and cucumber dip, cubes of feta, salsa, smoked oysters, chargrilled vegetables, olives, caperberries, slices of sausage, sprigs of fresh rosemary, freshly toasted crostini to use as a base for the dips. Let your imagination run wild!

red salmon and lite crème fraîche dip

210 g can red salmon, drained
2–3 tbsp lite crème fraîche
**1 tbsp chopped parsley or 2 tsp
  chopped dill**
fresh lemon juice
salt and freshly ground black pepper

Combine the drained fish with the other ingredients and season to taste.

You can substitute the salmon for tuna if desired.

yoghurt and cucumber dip

This is a superb dip to serve at your next barbecue with lamb loins or Grilled Root Vegetables (page 87). It is light and refreshing, and is even a happy partner to the humble meat pattie or grilled sausage. Try it and you will be delighted!

1 telegraph cucumber, grated
1 cup plain unsweetened yoghurt
2–3 cloves garlic, minced
20 fresh mint leaves, chopped finely
1 tbsp olive oil
juice of 1 lemon
¼ tsp cumin
½ tsp ground coriander
salt and freshly ground black pepper

Squeeze the grated cucumber in a tea towel to remove the excess liquid. In a bowl, mix all the ingredients, adding salt and pepper to taste. Cover and refrigerate until needed. Best eaten on the day it is made.

This is delicious as a sauce to accompany spiced beef in a pita bread.

It makes a superb low-fat accompaniment to salads instead of a dressing.

This works well as a cooling agent when eating spicy food.

antipasto platter

crostini

Crostini are so easy to make in advance for a party: slice a loaf of French bread and spray slices with olive oil. Place slices on an oven tray and bake at 180°C for 10 minutes or until golden in colour. Turn oven off and leave crostini in the oven overnight. Next day store the crostini in an airtight container or zip-lock bags – you can prepare these about a week beforehand if desired. They keep for a while, but if they have become a little 'stale', simply reheat in the oven to make them crispy again.

Our selection of crostini used cottage cheese as a base and then were topped with:

prawns, slices of capsicum and rocket
cucumber, rocket and smoked oysters
cherry tomatoes, onion and avocado

Cottage cheese is mild-tasting, with a fresh, slightly acidic flavour. With only 4% fat and a good source of protein, it's a sensible and delicious, low-fat option for home entertainers.

crostini

rustic warm crostini with tuna, lemon and capers

If you think snacking is unhealthy, then think again. These are the perfect accompaniment to a bowl of soup from a slow cooker during winter, or simply eaten alone during the warmer months. Tuna is packed full of goodness and protein – the ideal lunch for a busy person.

½ long loaf French bread, thickly
   sliced on the diagonal
¼ cup olive oil
2 garlic cloves
125 g black olives, pitted and cut into
   pieces
1 tbsp capers
8 semi-dried or sundried tomatoes
1 tbsp chopped fresh oregano
210 g can tuna in spring water,
   drained
1 cup wild rocket or salad greens
extra virgin olive oil for drizzling
freshly ground black pepper

Brush bread slices very lightly with olive oil and place on a preheated countertop grill. Grill for a few minutes until golden. Alternatively, place on a baking sheet and bake in an oven heated to 180°C oven for 8–10 minutes.

Halve a garlic clove and rub the cut-side over the bread while still hot.

Finely chop remaining garlic and place in a bowl with olives, capers, tomatoes and oregano. Add tuna, breaking up the pieces slightly as you mix. Place a few rocket or salad greens onto the warm bread and top with the tuna mix. Drizzle with oil and season with black pepper.

let dinner
begin

carrot soup with cucumber cashew relish

A colourful and tantalising soup.

SERVES 8
2 tbsp olive oil
1 large red onion, diced
10 carrots, chopped (about 4 cups)
3 cloves garlic, chopped
1 tsp sugar
½ tsp salt
½ tsp curry powder
pinch of cayenne pepper
5 cups water
1 tbsp lemon juice
1 tsp champagne vinegar

RELISH:
½ cup diced telegraph cucumber
½ cup freshly toasted cashew nuts
2 tbsp crystallized ginger, finely diced
1 tbsp chopped coriander
2 tsp chopped mint
¼ tsp salt

To make the soup, heat the oil in a large stockpot over a medium heat. Add the onion, carrots and garlic, and cook gently for 5 minutes. Add sugar, salt, curry powder and cayenne pepper, and cook for 1 minute. Add water, bring to the boil, then reduce to a simmer. Cover and simmer until carrots are tender – about 15 minutes. Purée soup in the a blender or food processor until smooth. Stir in lemon juice and vinegar. Ladle the soup into bowls and top with relish.

To make relish, combine all ingredients in a small bowl.

You can serve this soup either hot or cold and with or without the relish.

spicy fish soup

This is a super simple soup made easily in a wok or large stockpot.

SERVES 2–3
¼ onion, finely minced
olive oil
2 stems fresh lemongrass, finely
    chopped
1 fresh red chilli
1 tbsp fresh minced ginger
1 potato, peeled and diced
4 cups fish stock
2 cups low-fat milk
1 cup whole kernel corn
3–4 hoki fillets, cut into chunks
1 tbsp chopped coriander
salt and freshly ground pepper

With the a wok or stockpot on low, add the onion and olive oil. Cook onion gently until translucent, but not coloured. Add lemongrass, chilli and ginger, and cook for 1 minute. Add potato and toss through and cook for another minute. Add stock and cook gently, covered, until potato is soft. Add the milk, corn and fish. Heat through gently but do not boil. When the fish is cooked, add coriander and season with salt and pepper to taste.

spicy fish soup

slow cooker lamb shanks

One of great delights for the home cook is to come home after being stuck in traffic to a house full of luscious aromas with no fear of food being over-cooked. A slow cooker makes this possible. Lamb shanks always benefit from long, slow cooking – ideally the meat should simply fall from the bone. If the meat is hard to move away from the bone – cook them longer.

SERVES 4–5

¼ cup flour

1 tbsp mixed herbs

4–5 lamb shanks, at room temperature

1 onion, chopped

3 cloves garlic, roughly chopped

¾ cup port

2 carrots, peeled and roughly chopped

2 stalks celery, sliced and roughly chopped

2 medium potatoes or kumara, peeled and roughly chopped

¼ cup tomato paste

1 cup beef stock

2 tbsp fresh rosemary

1 tbsp brown sugar

Combine the flour with mixed herbs. Toss the shanks in the flour and place in slow cooker. Add all the remaining ingredients, including any remaining flour. Cover and cook on high for 5–6 hours or on low for 8–10 hours.

Use the leftover pulp from a juicer: the pulp from the spinach, carrot and celery juice could be used with the shanks instead of chopped vegetables.

If you are in a hurry, just cover the shanks with your favourite commercial pasta sauce, a slurp of wine, plus the leftover pulp from the juicer and this recipe will work just as well.

slow cooker lamb shanks

tandoori slow cooker chicken

SERVES 4

1 cup plain unsweetened yoghurt
1 tbsp curry paste
1.5 kg fresh chicken
500 g potatoes, peeled and cut into
    2.5 cm chunks

In a large bowl, combine the yoghurt and curry paste. Pour marinade over chicken, cover and place in fridge overnight.

Next morning, place potatoes in bottom of a slow cooker bowl. Remove chicken from marinade and place on top of the potatoes. Put cover on slow cooker and cook on low for 7–9 hours.

mum's chicken stew

My mother loves her slow cooker. She says after 55 years of cooking every night she often finds it hard to get enthusiastic about cooking dinners, so the slow cooker is the best solution. In the morning she prepares dinner by throwing some favourite ingredients into the slow cooker and leaving it on low all day. After 9 hours the aromas are just magic. All that is then needed is some rice cooked easily in a rice cooker, and a quick tossed salad. Best of all, the slow cooker takes simple ingredients such as chicken thighs and root vegetables and transforms them into a stunning stew, full of wonderful savoury flavours and super tender meat.

SERVES 6

3–4 potatoes, peeled and cut into
    chunks
1–2 kumara, peeled and cut into
    chunks
3 carrots, peeled and cut into chunks
1 onion, peeled and finely chopped
850 g–1 kg chicken thighs, roughly
    chopped into big chunks
2–3 garlic cloves, finely minced
2–3 tbsp fresh herbs (rosemary,
    parsley and thyme all work well)
salt and freshly ground black pepper
410 g can cream of chicken soup
a slurp of red wine (about ½ cup)

Place the first 3 ingredients in the slow cooker, then add the onion. Place chicken on top and then add the remaining ingredients. Cover and cook on low for 8–9 hours.

Serve with rice.

Do not lift the lid; every time you do you slow down the cooking process in a slow cooker by 30 minutes.

Once you have tried this recipe once or twice, experiment with lamb or pork pieces as well.

If the thought of peeling vegetables in the morning is too much, do it the night before, put them in the bowl of the slow cooker, cover and leave in the fridge. In the morning before work place the chicken on top of the vegetables and add other ingredients, then turn on the slow cooker.

shrimp salad with buttermilk dressing

A classic favourite with a modern twist.

SERVES 2
200 g peeled cocktail shrimp, drained
½ avocado, sliced
3–4 cups salad greens
2 tbsp red onion, finely chopped
¼ pawpaw, sliced
croutons to serve

Combine all the ingredients. Gently toss through a little dressing (below) and top with croutons.

buttermilk dressing

⅓ cup lite mayonnaise
⅓ cup cultured buttermilk
1 tsp lemon zest
1 tsp lemon juice
salt and freshly ground black pepper
   to taste
1 tbsp chopped chives
2 sundried tomatoes, finely chopped

Combine all the ingredients in a covered container. Store in the fridge and use within 5 days.

Croutons: spray cubed stale bread with olive oil and bake on a non-stick oven tray at 150°C till golden and crisp. Check after 20 minutes.

Most seafoods are low in carbohydrates – many have less than 0.5%.

mustard and herb glazed roast leg of lamb

When selecting a leg of lamb for the frypan, make sure it is not too big, as the cover must fit on the frypan.

SERVES 4–6
2 tbsp olive oil
2.5 kg leg of lamb at room temperature

GLAZE:
¼ cup Dijon mustard
2 tsp soy sauce
3 garlic cloves, minced
2 tsp chopped thyme
2 tsp chopped rosemary
1 tbsp chopped basil
1–2 tbsp olive oil
salt and freshly ground black pepper
   to taste

Heat olive oil in a non-stick frypan on a medium heat. Brown the lamb on all sides. Reduce heat to a low heat.

To make the glaze, combine all the ingredients.

Spoon glaze over the meat and pour 2 cups of water into the pan. Cover and cook for an additional 2 hours. Remove meat from pan and allow to rest for 15–20 minutes before carving.

If you want to cook your lamb in a regular oven, make glaze and smear over room-temperature lamb and roast (without the water) as per your usual method.

hoisin chicken stir-fry

It's super simple to make a delicious, fast dinner for the family with a wok. Hoisin sauce is available at the supermarket and makes this chicken stir-fry something special.

SERVES 4–6
3 tbsp peanut oil
1 medium onion, cut in half and sliced
1 red capsicum, deseeded and sliced
500 g boneless and skinless chicken breasts, cut into 2cm chunks
salt and freshly ground black pepper
150 g snow peas, trimmed
2 tsp minced fresh ginger
red chilli flakes, crushed
⅓ cup hoisin sauce
2 tbsp water
⅓ cup dry-roasted cashews, chopped

Heat 2 tbsp of the oil in a wok over medium heat. Add onion and cook for 2–3 minutes. Add capsicum and cook until lightly coloured – about 4 minutes. Remove vegetables from the wok; set aside.

Pour the remaining 1 tbsp of oil in the wok. Sprinkle the chicken with salt and pepper and add to the oil. Cook for about 2–8 minutes, stirring frequently, so that all sides brown. Stir in the snow peas and ginger. Sprinkle in some red chilli flakes. Reduce heat to medium low, then stir in hoisin sauce and water. Simmer for 1 minute to wilt the snow peas and finish cooking the chicken – but don't overdo it! Sprinkle with cashew nuts.

Great served with rice.

A rice cooker makes cooking rice easy and disaster-free. Or you can use a steamer to cook the rice as we did for the sushi recipe below.

sushi

Once you start working with a steamer, you will be hooked – enjoy the results with this sushi rice.

SERVES 4
1 cup short-grain sushi rice
2 cups water
1 sachet of powdered sushi mix
4 sheets nori (seaweed sheets)
1 sushi mat
½ carrot, grated and peeled
¼ telegraph cucumber, sliced into julienne strips
90 g can tuna in olive oil, drained
45 g can smoked mussels

Prepare a steamer according to the instructions. Place rice and water in the rice bowl and fit bowl on top of the steamer dish. Cover with lid and steam for 30 minutes.

Once finished, turn unit off at the wall. Sprinkle rice with sushi powder and fluff with a fork. Place lid back on the steamer and leave to cool.

Lay nori on sushi rolling mat. Cover ⅔ of the nori from top with a quarter of the rice, spreading it out and patting it down with damp hands. Make sure it is evenly spread to the edges. Wet your hands first – this makes it easier to spread out the rice. Place carrot, cucumber, tuna and or smoked mussels on rice.

Slightly moisten the top end of the nori and roll up tightly. Wrap rolls in plastic wrap and place in fridge. Slice into 8 pieces.

Serve with soy sauce, slices of pickled ginger and wasabi.

sushi

chilli stir-fried bok choy

Use a wok to make this dish quickly and effortlessly. We topped the bok choy with Grilled Herb Chicken.

SERVES 3–4

2 tsp sesame oil

1 tbsp peanut oil

1 capsicum, deseeded and sliced

1–2 long red chillies, deseeded and
  thinly sliced

1 tbsp grated fresh ginger

2–3 cloves garlic, crushed

2 bunches bok choy, trimmed and
  roughly chopped

2 tbsp soy sauce

1 tbsp sweet Thai chilli sauce

2 spring onions, thinly sliced

¼ cup toasted cashews, chopped

fresh herbs to garnish

Heat oils in a wok and add capsicum, chillies, ginger and garlic; stir-fry until capsicum is tender. Add bok choy and sauces; stir-fry until bok choy is wilted. Sprinkle with spring onions and nuts and garnish with fresh herbs.

Serve with grilled chicken or fish.

grilled herb chicken

Sometimes the best recipes are the simplest – a countertop grill produces a perfect result.

SERVES 2

2 chicken breasts, trimmed, cut into 4
  flat slices

1 tbsp wholeseed mustard

1 tbsp Dijon mustard

1 tbsp dry tarragon leaves

olive oil

Combine the chicken with the mustards and tarragon leaves. Marinate chicken for a minimum of 30 minutes or, ideally, overnight.

Preheat the grill for 3–5 minutes and spray with olive oil. Place chicken on grill, lower the lid and cook for 3–4 minutes or until tender.

chilli stir-fried bok choy and grilled herb chicken

health tip

Get more vitamin K! Several studies have
shown that vitamin K can help maintain
bone density and strength. Sources
include leafy green vegetables such as bok
choy and broccoli, and plant oils.

grilled vegetables made simple

Grilling vegetables is easy using a countertop grill. Simply preheat the grill for 3–5 minutes. Spray the grill lightly with oil, place vegetables on the grill and lower lid to ensure even cooking.

SERVES 4

1 small eggplant, sliced

1 courgette, deseeded and sliced diagonally

1 red capsicum, deseeded and sliced

1 yellow capsicum, deseeded and sliced

salt for seasoning

olive oil for spraying

1 cup olive oil

1 tsp salt

1 tsp chopped parsley

2 tsp crushed garlic

freshly ground black pepper

1 tbsp lemon juice

Season the vegetables with salt and spray very lightly with oil, if desired. Grill, then remove when lightly coloured. When cool, place in a bowl with the rest of the ingredients

Serve topped with steamed fish, grilled chicken or slices of lean, grilled beef, and drizzled with your favourite low-fat dressing.

health tip

Frozen fish fillets are a convenient way to serve fish to your family. High in protein and a rich source of omega-3 fatty acids, fish is an important ingredient to help keep your cardiovascular system in good shape.

grilled vegetables with hoki

steamed fish in white wine

Use baking paper to make these small fish parcels – a luscious, yet healthy dinner option for the family. Defrost hoki fillets in the fridge the morning you want to serve the fish – place on paper towels and cover with plastic wrap.

SERVES 4
⅓ **cup dry white wine**
3 tbsp capers, chopped
3 tbsp chopped mint
2 large tomatoes, finely chopped
4 hoki fillets, defrosted
¼ **tsp salt**
freshly ground black pepper
4 thin slices lemon

COUSCOUS:
1½ **cups boiling water**
1 tbsp butter
salt and freshly ground black pepper
1½ **cups couscous**
2–3 tbsp fresh herbs, chopped (mint, coriander, basil, thyme and parsley all work well)
2–3 tbsp of your favourite fresh herb dressing (optional)

Turn on the steamer.

Combine wine, capers, mint and tomatoes. Season fish with salt and pepper. Place each fillet of fish in centre of 4 pieces of baking paper. Spoon over tomato mixture and top with a lemon slice. Fold parcel up and place in steamer for 15–20 minutes or until just cooked.

To prepare couscous, make according to the packet directions. Season to taste and add fresh herbs.

Place the couscous on a platter and top with fish fillets. Drizzle over liquid from parcels. You can also drizzle a little fresh herb salad dressing over if you feel the dish needs more liquid.

seafood pasta

You can avoid a heavy cream sauce when making seafood pasta – think olive oil, herbs and garlic with seafood rather than cream and butter. These Mediterranean flavours showcase the seafood perfectly and it's not complicated.

SERVES 4
water
250 g fettuccine or spaghetti
salt
¼–⅓ cup extra virgin olive oil
3–4 cloves garlic, finely minced
2 tsp freshly grated ginger
2 fresh tomatoes, diced
4 hoki fillets, cut into chunks
½–1 cup chopped fresh herbs
(parsley, thyme, basil, coriander
and dill all work well)
¼ cup sweet Thai chilli sauce
juice of 1 lemon
2 tsp finely grated lemon zest
salt and freshly ground black pepper
3 cups assorted seafood
1–2 spring onions, finely chopped

Heat a large pot of water and when boiling add the pasta and salt. Cook pasta according to the directions on the packet.

While the pasta is cooking, heat a little of the oil in a wok and cook the garlic, ginger and tomatoes. Add the fish and cook for several minutes to medium-rare. If using mussels lightly heat through with the fish.

When the pasta is 'al dente', drain (leaving a little pasta water to one side) and add to wok. Drizzle with most of the olive oil and stir through the fresh herbs, sweet Thai chilli sauce, lemon juice and zest. Season with salt and pepper while the pasta is hot.

Add any other cooked or prepared seafood of your choice, plus a little drizzle of olive oil and a little of the pasta water to give the dish extra 'sauce', if needed. Sprinkle with spring onions and season if desired.

You can use a variety of products: the marinated classic mussels (drain from the brine), smoked mussels or oysters, drained canned tuna or salmon, shrimps and crab.

cranberry dairy cocktail

Research has shown that drinking cranberry juice is good for your health, so why not make these cocktails and enjoy healthy drinks with friends and family at any time.

SERVES 2–3
½ fresh lime, roughly chopped
½ cup plain unsweetened yoghurt
1–2 tsp liquid honey
3–4 fresh mint leaves
ice
1 cup cranberry juice

Place the first five ingredients into a blender and process. With the motor running, slowly pour in the cranberry juice.

lamb fillet bacon wraps

A countertop grill is perfect for grilling lamb fillets. Preheat for 3–5 minutes. The 'ready' light will illuminate. Spray the grill lightly with oil, place meat on the grill and lower lid to ensure even cooking.

SERVES 4
8 lamb fillets
8 tsp wholegrain mustard
8 bacon strips
salad greens
grilled root vegetables (see page 87)
1 cup herb yoghurt dressing
   (see below)

DRESSING:
1 cup plain unsweetened yoghurt
¼ cup chopped fresh herbs (parsley,
   chives, mint and oregano work
   well)
squeeze of lemon juice
salt and freshly ground black pepper

Take the lamb fillets out of the fridge and let them warm to room temperature before cooking. Remove any sinew or silverskin from the fillets. Smear each fillet with mustard and wrap the bacon around the fillets. Cook on very hot grill for approximately 2–3 minutes per side. Leave to rest for a few minutes while you assemble the salad and the precooked grilled root vegetables.

Slice the lamb fillets on the diagonal and place on top of the grilled root vegetables.

Drizzle with the herb yoghurt dressing and serve.

To make the yoghurt dressing, combine yoghurt with fresh herbs, lemon juice, and salt and pepper to taste.

pasta with mint pesto, tuna and sundried tomatoes

SERVES 2–3
250 g penne
⅓ cup mint pesto (see page 84)
⅓ cup sundried tomatoes, drained
   and chopped
210 g can tuna in olive oil
salt and freshly ground black pepper
2 tsp balsamic vinegar
½ cup freshly grated Parmesan

Cook pasta according to the packet instructions. Drain pasta well, reserving ⅓ cup of the pasta water.

Transfer the pasta to a large bowl. Add the reserved pasta water, the pesto, sundried tomatoes, tuna, and salt and pepper. Toss to combine. Drizzle with balsamic vinegar and serve immediately. Pass around the Parmesan separately to sprinkle on top.

Purists will tell you that you do not combine seafood and Parmesan but it works well in this recipe. Feta is also delicious with this combination.

Seafood is heart-healthy food from nearly every dietary perspective. High in protein and low in carbohydrates and cholesterol, most varieties are also low in fat. The fat present is beneficial due to the omega-3 fatty acid content. The oils in fish are rich in unsaturated fatty acids which tend to lower plasma lipids and cholesterol.

lamb fillet bacon wraps on grilled
vegetables

mint pesto

With mint pesto on hand you can transform even a simple baked potato into something quite special. Instead of sour cream you can place a spoonful of plain unsweetened yoghurt inside a baked potato and a little mint pesto on top. It is equally scrumptious over pasta.

MAKES 1½ CUPS
½ cup pine nuts
6 cloves garlic
3 cups fresh mint leaves
1 cup olive oil
juice of 1 lemon
salt and freshly ground black pepper
   to taste

Place the pine nuts and garlic in a blender or food processor fitted with a steel blade and process to a paste. Add the mint and process until finely chopped.

With the machine running, drizzle in the oil in a thin, steady stream. Add the lemon juice and salt and pepper to taste, and process until blended.

You can also combine this pesto with plain unsweetened yoghurt as a dipping sauce for grilled vegetables or as an accompaniment to grilled lamb on a bed of couscous.

healthy polenta

A nutritious and low-fat option for the whole family.

SERVES 3–4
2½ cups low-fat milk
1 cup water
20 g butter
1 cup instant polenta
fresh herbs, such as parsley, thyme
   and rosemary
salt and freshly ground black pepper

Heat the milk, water and butter in a saucepan over medium heat. When simmering, pour in polenta in a thin stream. Whisk for 5 minutes to combine and to remove any lumps.

Add chopped fresh herbs and season with salt and pepper to taste.

Let the polenta cool, then place into lamington tin, lined with baking paper and smooth over.

When cold, cut into triangles, spray lightly with olive oil and grill in a countertop grill until golden in colour.

We served these grilled polenta triangles topped with steamed chicken (allow 35–40 minutes cooking time in a steamer) and drizzled with a pesto sauce. For the pesto sauce, we simply added extra lemon juice and a little olive oil to a generous spoonful of pesto.

polenta with chicken and pesto sauce

steamed and grilled vegetables
with mint pesto and yoghurt
dipping sauce

lemon and toasted poppy seed dressing

This recipe is from Hawke's Bay chef Jenny Parton – and is scrumptious over steamed chicken and grilled polenta.

½ cup poppy seeds
2 garlic cloves
1 spring onion
2 tbsp Dijon mustard
1 egg
200 ml white wine vinegar
1 tsp turmeric powder
4 tbsp lemon juice
750 ml soya oil
salt and freshly ground black pepper

Toast the poppy seeds in a hot, dry, non-stick frypan until fragrant. Allow to cool. Place the garlic, spring onion, mustard, egg, vinegar, turmeric and lemon juice into a blender and combine. Add the oil in a slow stream until emulsified. Season to taste with salt and pepper, then mix through the toasted poppy seeds.

grilled root vegetables

A countertop grill is perfect for grilling root vegetables. Preheat for 3–5 minutes. Spray the grill lightly with oil, place vegetables on the grill and lower lid to ensure even cooking.

SERVES 4
4 potatoes, peeled and cut into 1.25 cm
    slices
3 kumara, peeled and cut into 1.25 cm
    slices
olive oil
2–4 sprigs fresh rosemary
sea salt
salt and freshly ground black pepper

Preheat the grill. Par-cook the potatoes and kumara in a large bowl suitable for the microwave. Do not add any liquid. Cover with plastic wrap and microwave on high for 5 minutes. Alternatively, boil until just tender.

Place the vegetables on the grill and lightly spray with olive oil, if desired. Scatter fresh rosemary over the top of the vegetables prior to grilling. Season with salt and pepper as you cook.

cook's tip

Use plain unsweetened yoghurt as a refreshing dipping sauce with your favourite steamed and grilled vegetables. Simply top a bowl of yoghurt with mint pesto (see page 84) for a zingy taste.

sweet chilli and lime dressing

Top Hawke's Bay chef Jenny Parton has a solid and well-deserved reputation for great flavours and stunning food. On a flight from Invercargill once, we started talking about low-fat dressings that give punchy flavour and she willingly shared her personal favourites for us all to enjoy.

2 tbsp black mustard seeds
2 spring onions, finely chopped
½ cup chopped coriander
1 cup lime juice
2 tsp sesame oil
½ cup oyster sauce
2 cups sweet Thai chilli sauce
1 tbsp garam masala

Toast the mustard seeds in a dry, hot non-stick frypan until they pop.

Combine all the remaining ingredients. This dressing will keep for several weeks in the fridge.

The lime juice can be replaced by lemon juice.

Make this dressing and give some away to friends. It is perfect with roasted pumpkin or fish.

tamarind dressing

This dressing is fantastic with any seafood or chicken.

½ cup brown sugar
3 tbsp fish sauce
4 tbsp tamarind juice
1 tbsp lemon juice
½–1 tbsp chilli paste
170 ml lite coconut cream

Combine all the ingredients.

and so to dessert

simple rice pudding

SERVES 3–4
½ cup short-grain rice
4½ cups low-fat milk
¼ cup sugar
¼ cup coconut threads (optional)
freshly grated nutmeg

Place rice, milk, sugar and coconut in a well-greased baking dish. Sprinkle grated nutmeg over pudding. Cook in a slow oven at 150°C for 2 hours.

Serve with natural yoghurt and spiced rhubarb cooked in a slow cooker or toasted coconut threads and a fruit salsa of pawpaw, rock melon and kiwifruit.

fruit salsa

SERVES 2–4
1 cup chopped kiwifruit (skin removed)
1 cup chopped pawpaw (skin removed)
1 cup chopped rock melon (skin removed)
2 tbsp finely chopped mint
a generous squeeze of lemon or lime juice
4 tbsp toasted coconut threads

Mix together and serve.

cook's tip

To toast coconut threads, simply place in a heated non-stick frypan and toss until lightly coloured.

simple rice pudding
and fruit salsa

slow cooker spiced rhubarb

SERVES 3–4
750 g rhubarb, cut into 2 cm pieces
¾ cup sugar
½ tsp cinnamon
3 whole cloves
1 tsp orange zest or lemon zest

Place all the ingredients in a slow cooker, cover and cook on low for 4–6 hours.

slow cooker poached pears

SERVES 3–4
2 cups dry red wine
1 cup sugar
6–8 medium pears, peeled
4 thick strips lemon rind

Place the wine and sugar into a slow cooker. Cover and cook on high until sugar is dissolved. Place pears into the slow cooker, turning to coat well with sugar syrup. Add lemon rind. Cover and cook on low for 5–6 hours or on high for 3–4 hours, turning occasionally to coat.

Serve with lite crème fraîche or spiced yoghurt (add a little crystallized ginger and spice to yoghurt). It's also good with lite sour cream mixed with 1 tbsp brown sugar per ½ cup sour cream.

grilled summer fruit with citrus passionfruit cream

Simply keep your countertop grill beside your bowl of summer stone fruit and you have an instant dessert.

SERVES 4
8 ripe nectarines
8 ripe apricots
½ cup orange juice or brandy
4 tbsp sugar
icing sugar for dusting

CITRUS PASSIONFRUIT CREAM:
250 g lite crème fraîche
3 tbsp lemon curd or fresh orange juice (optional)
4 fresh passionfruit or 3 tbsp passionfruit pulp

Preheat the grill for 3–5 minutes. Spray grill plates with cooking spray.

Cut the apricots and nectarines in half and remove the stones. Place on the grill with the cut-side up. Drizzle with brandy or orange juice, and sprinkle with sugar. Lower the lid and grill on high until the sugar starts to caramelize (allow about 10 minutes). Sprinkle fruit with icing sugar.

While the fruit is grilling make the citrus passionfruit cream. Combine the lite crème fraîche with the lemon curd or orange juice, and the passionfruit. Place in a bowl or side dish to accompany the platter of warm grilled fruits.

For interesting texture, serve with biscotti or home-made cookies.

The bonus here is that you can prepare the cream as the fruit is grilling. A dessert has never been so easy!

Any leftover passionfruit cream can be placed in the freezer and it will become instant ice cream.

grilled summer fruit with
citrus passionfruit cream

healthy fruit crumble

Use a food processor to slice the apples and then make the crumble. Healthy eating should be this easy and stress-free!

Fruit crumble can be an effective and healthy way of increasing your daily fruit intake. Use apples and blackberries, or peaches and redcurrants – berries are rich in antioxidants and fibre.

Add as little sugar as possible to sweeten. Always have more fruit than crumble, and in the crumble use oats and a little sugar and butter. Oats and apples contain a high level of soluble fibre, which can be helpful in reducing blood cholesterol and lowering blood pressure.

SERVES 4
4–5 large apples, peeled
½ cup Craisins or blueberries (fresh or frozen)
squeeze of lemon juice
3–4 tbsp brown sugar
drizzle of maple syrup, passionfruit syrup or apple syrup (optional)
½ cup rolled oats
1 cup flour
½ cup coconut threads
generous piece of orange zest
2 tbsp brown sugar
1 tsp cinnamon
150 g butter

Preheat oven to 180°C. Place the peeled apples in a food processor and slice. Place the slices into a greased baking dish with the berries. Squeeze the lemon juice over the fruit and sprinkle the first measure of brown sugar over the fruit. Drizzle over syrup (if using).

Place the oats in the food processor and, with the motor running, add the flour, coconut, orange zest, second measure of brown sugar, cinnamon and butter. Process until crumbly, however don't over-process once the butter is added.

Scatter crumble over the fruit and bake for 50–60 minutes.

Serve with yoghurt and/or custard.

Craisins are sweetened dried cranberries, available at supermarkets.

index